Alexandra and the Awful, Awkward, No Fun, Truly Bad Dates

Thadd, 29

Your dreams

6 foot cuz you'll ask. Winnin' at brunch.
Work hard, play hard. Not your pen pal.

Todd, 31

Gone fishin'

A reel catch. Looking to fall for
someone hook, line, and sinker!

Marc, 33

Your next adventure

Road-warrior living life at 35,000 feet.
Looking to share my airline miles and
adventures.

Alexandra and the Awful, Awkward, No Fun, Truly Bad Dates

Rebekah Manley

Illustrated by Catarina Oliveira

Karl, 34

Always outdoors

Believe in love at first swipe? On the app to get off this app. Let's go on a hike.

Patrick, 28

At your service

"Man of the year. He'll make you dinner and smile. He's a keeper." —my Mom

ULYSSES PRESS

Published in the United States by:
Ulysses Press
P.O. Box 3440
Berkeley, CA 94703
www.ulyssespress.com

ISBN: 978-1-64604-066-7
Library of Congress Control Number: 2020935715

Printed in China by JHP through Four Colour Print Group
10 9 8 7 6 5 4 3 2 1

Acquisitions editor: Claire Sielaff
Managing editor: Claire Chun
Editor: Renee Rutledge
Front cover design: Jake Flaherty
Illustrations: Catarina Oliveira
Photographs on page 32: author © Danielle Selby; illustrator
   © Catarina Oliveira

I dedicate this first book to my team of family and friends. Writing and dating are not solitary sports. No matter the score, you've loved me, listened through heartache, cheered fiercely, and kept me laughing. Thank you for believing in me.

For all those going on awful, awkward, no fun, truly bad dates—know you are not alone. I hope this book keeps you laughing.

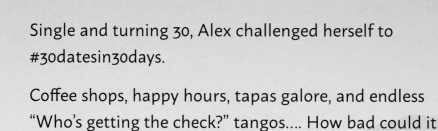

Single and turning 30, Alex challenged herself to #30datesin30days.

Coffee shops, happy hours, tapas galore, and endless "Who's getting the check?" tangos.... How bad could it be? And what did she have to lose?

Number 1 was clearly a #miSTEAK.

Her date insisted she get prime rib—and that women should just accept the wage gap. "Your brains are just different," he mansplained. Alex grabbed her steak to go and let him enjoy the financial success of buying her meal.

Date number 2 briefed everyone at the wine and cheese bar on his Ivy League status! #HarvardHavarti tossed his menu at the server—"I can't believe you don't have a proper dessert wine."

Alex deserted him.

Guess who treated Mom to a cruise every year? Number 3. They even lived next door to each other in matching apartments. Before Alex took her first bite, #3 posted a photo and tagged his mom. "Look, mac and cheese with lobster—your favorite." #MomIsYourLobster

His mom double tapped.

Alex tapped out.

She received AWFUL reception from number 4. They met online and that's where he stayed. He had his phone out their entire date. #PhoneItIn #LossofAPPetite

Numbers 5–7 were like cereal without a prize. Perfectly fine, but not worth a round two. #ChexPlease

It felt like work to hear some dates ONLY talk about their jobs.

Alex appreciated number 8's preparation until he demanded silence to perfect his copper theory. #CuNever #NoChemistry

Number 9 spent the whole date teaching his favorite programming languages. He permitted questions but didn't reciprocate. #DoesNotCompute

Alex felt hopeful about number 10…

Until he lectured her on Russian classics. "If you're not reading the best," he told her. "Why read at all?" Too bad he couldn't read her face. #AcademiNAH

Numbers 11, 12, AND 16 were AWKWARD and so hurt when she didn't trust them enough to go to their place for the "first date." Those nights she treated herself, and her gut instinct, to a double-decker strawberry cone. #IceCreamForPersonalSafety #ReadyToTasteRomance

Alex thought she had a coffee date with number 13.
Instead, she was served a green-tea lecture and a bite-
by-bite calorie count of her blueberry yogurt muffin.
#ReadyForADateDiet

Date 15 had zero aspirations of travel or fun in general. "I prefer to stay in my own neighborhood. Everything I need to see is on YouTube."

As he talked, Alex imagined a far-off land, one full of exciting possibilities and people with actual personalities. #DreamingOfAustralia

Numbers 14, 17, and 19 were NO FUN and made her grateful for caffeine.

"Of course I want to hear about the time you got your wisdom teeth removed."

"Your closet is made up entirely of plaid shirts and chinos? Fascinating."

"I've never thought mulch about dirt varieties."

Alex went back for extra shots, just to stay awake. #ALatteSmallTalk

Alex felt like she was babysitting #18. He burped the alphabet and literally skated out on the check. She wanted to send a bill to his parents. #NoMoreDateCare

#DrunkDates barely counted—Alex never met number 20. He was too intoxicated to find the restaurant. The next day, Mr. 21 lost track of Long Islands and passed out at the table.

It was strange to attend a first date's birthday, but Alex figured it would be fun to meet number 22's friends. The surprise party was on them as her TRULY BAD date "gifted" them the "opportunity" to invest in his startup. New rule: #NoMorePartyFavors.

#FortheBooks (or not) 23 and 24 had all the advice:

"You haven't invested in Bitcoin? You're missing out on the future!" "I can't believe you like books! Print is dead. I could fit all of the Library of Congress on my phone." Alex decided to leave both of them on read.

EVERY FRIDAY NIGHT

SHOT NIGHT

LADIES

FREE BODY SHOTS
FOR THE RIGHT BODY

BEER FESTIVAL

LiVe sic

ENTRANCE

Alex showed up to number 25's "favorite spot" and unfortunately, all the signs pointed to another awful, awkward, no fun, truly bad date.

Numbers 26–29...Alex texted her friends:
#DONTEVENASK #NotWorthIt #MovingtoAustralia

As #30datesin30days was coming to an end, Alex was at the end of her rope.

She was 30, single, and almost thirty dates clearer on what she did (and did NOT) want. With only one date to go, Alex was expecting the worst...

But #NoShow number 30 was her best date yet. "I'll take one of everything," she told the server.

It was so good, in fact, that she was ready for #30datesin30days again. Rock climbing, hikes, trips to the winery, dancing, traveling...

With herself.

And maybe a few fab friends.

There would be no more awful, awkward, no fun, truly bad dates now that Alex learned how to #SelfValiDATE.

Especially in Australia.
#KoalaMeFabulous

About the Author

Rebekah Manley holds her master of fine arts in children's literature from Hollins University and feels like she's earned her MFA in dating. She lives in Austin, Texas, and is fueled by swimming, queso, and good conversation. Rebekah runs the Texas Center for the Book and works to encourage literacy, reading, and library use in the Lone Star State. You can read more at rebekahmanley.com and on her blog bravetutu.com. Please connect on Twitter: @RebekahAManley and Instagram: @RebekahAManley & @YourBraveTutu.

About the Illustrator

Catarina Oliveira is a Portuguese illustrator living in Toronto, Canada. After graduating in graphic design and working ten years in the design industry, she redirected her career path to do what she loves—creating characters and illustrating stories, particularly for children's books. When she is not drawing, she enjoys being at home, cooking (but not baking), and going on hiking trips around the world. You can see her work at catarinaoliveirastudio.com and on Instagram: @catarinaoliveirastudio.